The GALAXY GUIDES

WHAT DOES GRAVITY DO?

Alix Wood

PowerKiDS press

Published in 2016 by **Rosen Publishing**
29 East 21st Street, New York, NY 10010

Editor: Eloise Macgregor
Designer: Alix Wood
Consultant: Kevin E. Yates, Fellow of the Royal Astronomical Society

Photo Credits: Cover, 1, 10, 11, 12, 13 top, 21 top, 22, 23 top, 27 top © NASA; 4 , 13 middle © Shutterstock; 5, 6 bottom, 7 top, 8, 9, 14, 15, 16, 17, 18, 19, 23 bottom, 24-25, 26 © Dollar Photo Club; 7 bottom © NASA/ Faith Fashion & Photos LLC; 11 top © Ute Kraus; 20 © NASA/Edward G Gibson; 21 bottom © NASA/JAXA; 25 top © DoD/Lt. Bryan Fetter; 25 middle © DoD/Pablo Jara Meza; 27 bottom © Alex Alishevskikh

Cataloging-in-Publication Data

Wood, Alix.
What does gravity do? / by Alix Wood.
p. cm. — (The galaxy guides)
Includes index.
ISBN 978-1-4994-0856-0 (pbk.)
ISBN 978-1-4994-0854-6 (6 pack)
ISBN 978-1-4994-0852-2 (library binding)
1. Gravity — Juvenile literature.
2. Force and energy — Juvenile literature.
I. Wood, Alix. II. Title.
QC178.W66 2016
531'.14—d23

Manufactured in the United States of America

CPSIA Compliance Information: Batch #: WS15PK
For Further Information contact Rosen Publishing, New York, New York at 1-800-237-9932

Contents

What Is Gravity? 4
Who Discovered Earth Has Gravity? 6
What Is Weight? What Is Mass? 8
How Did Gravity Help Shape the Universe? 10
Could One Big Mass Attract Everything? 12
How Does Gravity Make Objects Go into Orbit? 14
How Does Gravity Affect Us on Earth? 16
How Does the Moon's Gravity Affect Earth? 18
How Do Astronauts Cope with Less Gravity? 20
Do Astronauts Float or Free-fall in Space? 22
What Is G-Force? 24
Could Gravity Cause an Object to Hit Earth? 26
Galaxy Quiz 28
Glossary 30
Further Information 31
Index and Answers 32

What Is Gravity?

Gravity is the force that causes objects to move toward each other. All objects have gravity, but how much depends on how much **mass** an object has. Mass is how much matter something has, not just how big something is. Objects with a large mass, like Earth or the Sun, have a strong gravitational pull.

Gravity is why things don't fall off a ball-shaped Earth!

HANDS-ON SCIENCE

What Does a Gravity Force Feel Like?

You will need: a tennis ball, a rubber band

Wrap a rubber band around a tennis ball. Put your finger between the ball and the rubber band and try to move your finger away from the ball. The rubber band is acting a little like gravity. It is pulling your finger back toward the center of the ball. Try to move your finger all around the ball. The gravity works with the same force all around.

Gravity is very important for us on Earth. Without Earth's gravity everything would float around unless we strapped it down! If you hit a baseball, it would fly off forever. Living with less gravity might be fun for a little while, but life would become difficult.

People's health suffers in space when there is hardly any gravity. Astronauts who have spent a long time in space have noticed their bones and muscles start to become weaker.

Who Discovered Earth Has Gravity?

A famous story says English mathematician Sir Isaac Newton was sitting in an apple orchard one evening. An apple fell from a tree onto the ground nearby. This apple got Newton thinking.

Newton began to realize that things did not just fall down. They were pulled down toward the center of Earth. Without the force of gravity everything would float around. No one had truly understood this before. His discovery was very important in helping people's understanding of the movements of the planets and the Sun, too.

a painting of Sir Isaac Newton

Before people understood how gravity worked it would have been hard to imagine that Earth was shaped like a ball. Why didn't people fall off the bottom? Once people knew that gravity held us to Earth then it was easier to imagine that people could live all around the planet!

HANDS-ON SCIENCE

Static Electricity Experiments That Work Like Gravity

You will need: a balloon, a household tap

Blow up the balloon. Run the tap to get a little stream of water. Hold the balloon near the water. Does anything happen to the direction of the stream? Now try rubbing the balloon on your hair. This creates **static electricity** – beware, your hair may stand on end! Now try moving the balloon close to the stream of water. Do you notice anything happening to the direction of the stream? You should find that the water is attracted to the balloon by the static electricity. This is like the effect Earth's gravity has when it pulls objects toward its center.

the flow of water moves toward the balloon

What Is Weight? What Is Mass?

Mass is how much matter an object has. People often incorrectly use the word "weight" to mean "mass." Weight is actually a measure of how strongly gravity pulls down on something.

Because gravity is pretty much the same everywhere on Earth, the two things are often the same. Objects with a large mass will have a large weight. If you could travel in space, your mass would stay the same from planet to planet, but your weight would depend on how the gravity of that planet pulls on you.

HANDS-ON SCIENCE

Fool Your Scales!

You will need: bathroom scales with a dial hand, not digital scales

Some scales can be fooled. Because they measure any downward force they don't know if that is gravity or some other force. Step on a bathroom spring scale that has a dial hand that spins around. Very gently jump up and down on the scale. Jump so your feet barely leave the scale, so you don't damage it! You will see your **apparent weight** change, while your mass stays the same. In space, without the force of gravity you would weigh nothing at all, but you are still the same shape and size and mass!

?

FACT FILE

If You Want to Lose Weight, Go to Space!

In space where there is zero gravity, an elephant would weigh nothing at all! On the Moon, where gravity is less strong than on Earth, a tiger would weigh around the weight of a cat! You can even get very slight differences in weight in different locations on Earth because the gravity varies slightly. If you weighed 100 pounds at the North Pole on a spring scale, at the **equator** you would weigh 5.5 ounces less! The equator is the imaginary line around the center of Earth halfway between the North and South Pole.

If weight and mass are different, why are they both weighed in pounds or kilograms? Scales show pounds or kilograms because that is what people understand best. Weight should really be weighed in **Newtons**, the unit used for measuring force. One pound is equal to around 4.45 Newtons. One kg is 9.81 Newtons. If you weighed 100 pounds (45.3 kg) you would be around 445 Newtons. Can you figure out your weight in Newtons?

How Did Gravity Help Shape the Universe?

Gravity is responsible for making the Universe the way it is. It is the force that helps matter group together and creates objects such as planets, moons, and stars.

new stars forming

A new star is formed when dust particles form a dense, spinning cloud. The cloud's core attracts more dust. The more mass it gets, the greater its gravitational pull gets. Eventually the cloud of dust and gas collapses in on itself and spins even faster. The temperature inside the cloud gets very hot. This energy sets off **nuclear reactions** releasing enormous bursts of energy. The cloud becomes a glowing star.

Planets and asteroids formed in a similar way to stars, but because they were made of less gas and dust, they did not heat up under the pressure of their own gravity

FACT FILE

What Objects in Space Have the Strongest Gravity?

A **black hole** has incredibly strong gravity. We can't see black holes. They pull any light near them into their center. The light cannot escape, so they are totally dark. That is how they got their name! We only know they exist because scientists can see the effect of their strong gravity on everything around them. They are formed when a massive star runs out of fuel and its layers of gas press down on itself, forcing the star to get smaller and smaller. As the star **condenses** its gravity increases. It becomes a black hole.

Could One Big Mass Attract Everything?

If a massive object in space attracts everything around it, why does everything in the Universe not all clump together in the same place? That is because gravity's strength becomes weaker over distance.

Sir Isaac Newton noticed the strength of Earth's gravity depended on how far objects were from the Earth's center. Scientists have **theories** about why this happens. Some scientists think everything with mass makes tiny particles called **gravitons**, which are responsible for the pull of gravity. The more mass something has, the more gravitons it has. Gravitons exist like a cloud around an object. The farther away from the object you go, the less effect the gravitons have. As they are invisible and have no mass, no one has proved gravitons actually exist though!

an artist's drawing of a black hole surrounded by gravitons

Space is bendy! Any object with mass pushes on space and bends it, so that other objects moving in a straight line go around the object at the same time. It looks like the larger object (right) is pulling the smaller object, but really it is bending space that causes the attraction!

HANDS-ON SCIENCE

Make a Model of How Space Curves

You will need: A marble, two small rocks, one with slightly more mass than the other, a dish towel, two friends to help

With a friend, stretch the dish towel flat by holding the corners tightly. Ask another friend to roll a marble from one end to the other. The marble should roll in a straight line across the flat surface. Now place a rock in the center. What happens now when you roll the marble across the dish towel? The rock's mass has deformed space and pulls the marble toward it. Try placing the second rock on the dish towel. Can you make the marble fall toward the smaller rock? How?

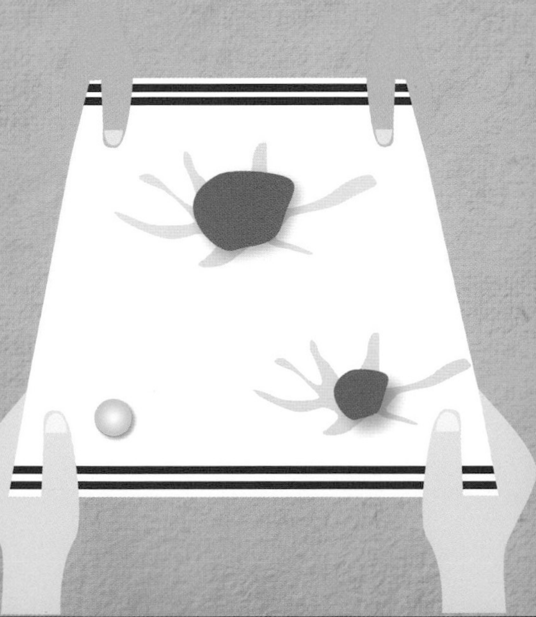

How Does Gravity Make Objects Go into Orbit?

The journey around an object in space is called an **orbit**. Objects in space are pulled into orbit by another object's gravitational pull. The more mass an object has, the stronger the pull it has. In our solar system the Sun has the largest mass, so everything travels in orbit around the Sun.

The Sun

Our solar system. The planets are not to scale.

An orbit happens when an object follows the curve of a planet or star. Gravity holds the object close to it, and keeps it from disappearing off into space. If an enormous cannon on top of an enormous mountain fired a cannonball using low power (A), the ball would curve down and hit Earth. Increase the power to just the right force (B), and the ball follows a path around Earth. This is because Earth is round, so the ground curves away from the ball, and Earth's gravity keeps the ball from going into space.

A

B

HANDS-ON SCIENCE

Make Your Own Orbit

You will need: a length of string, a tennis ball, an open space

Tie the string tightly around the tennis ball. Hold the string away from your body and start to swing it around in a circle. As the ball circles you it is constantly being pulled toward you, like the Sun's gravity pulls on Earth. The sideways motion causes the ball to keep moving around in an orbit. Without the sideways motion the ball would be pulled to the center. What would happen if gravity stopped working? Let go of the string and see.

How Does Gravity Affect Us on Earth?

Gravity is very important to life on Earth. The Sun's gravity keeps our planet orbiting around the Sun. Without the Sun's light and heat everything on Earth would die. Earth's gravity holds things in place on Earth. Importantly, it keeps our **atmosphere** close to the planet. Earth's atmosphere creates the rain for our crops and the air we breathe.

Everything that lives on our planet has become very used to the strength of gravity that exists here. A change in the amount of strength would be difficult for living things to adjust to.

Does Gravity Pull Everything the Same?

You will need: a camera phone or video camera, two unbreakable objects of different weights, a friend, a stepladder

In 1589, Italian scientist Galileo Galilei was the first to realize that gravity pulls objects of different weights at the same speed toward Earth. He dropped two objects from the top of the Leaning Tower of Pisa (left). You might think that the heavier object would hit ground first. Try this experiment and see for yourself. Carefully climb a ladder with the two objects. Ask your friend to start the video camera. Drop the two objects. Did one hit the ground before the other or did they hit at the same time? The only thing that could slow one object down more than another is **air resistance**. Air resistance is how a parachute slows down a person falling to Earth. The shape of the parachute fills with air and slows it down while it falls. A feather would fall slower because it acts a little like a parachute.

FACT FILE

Gravity Makes You Shorter!

Did you know that every day you are taller in the morning than you are at night? At the end of the day you are about 1/2 inch (1.25 cm) shorter than when you got up that morning. Ask someone to measure you when you get up in the morning and then again before you go to bed and you should see a difference. This happens because of gravity. All day, gravity is pulling you toward the center of Earth, squashing your spine. Lying down at night allows your spine to stretch back to your full height.

How Does the Moon's Gravity Affect Earth?

Just as the Sun's strong gravity pulls Earth into orbit around it, Earth's gravity pulls the Moon into orbit around Earth. Earth's gravity is six times stronger than the Moon's gravity. The Moon pulls on Earth too, though, just not as strongly. The Moon's pull affects Earth in a few ways.

You can see the effect of the Moon on Earth in the ocean's tides. The Moon's gravity pulls on Earth's oceans and **distorts** them, causing tides. The water on the side of Earth closest to the Moon experiences the biggest pull, and bulges outward. The water on the opposite side also bulges. As Earth rotates, the Moon is over different parts of Earth causing the swell to move around the planet.

FACT FILE

Why Doesn't the Moon Get Pulled Down to Earth?

If our gravity is stronger than the Moon's, why doesn't the Moon get pulled toward Earth? Actually, the Moon is falling all the time. It doesn't get any closer to us because it is falling around us in an orbit. It acts a little like a ball on the end of a piece of string swung around in a circle. If you cut the string the ball would fly off. If there were suddenly no gravity on Earth, the Moon would fly off in a similar way.

If there were no Moon, a day on Earth would be much shorter. The **friction** caused by the Moon is very gradually slowing down Earth's rotation. The change is very tiny, but if Earth had never had a Moon, the length of a day on Earth would be around 6-8 hours long!

Earth spins around on its **axis**. It is tilted at 23.5 degrees. It stays at that angle because the Moon's gravity holds it in place. Without that pull from the Moon, Earth would wobble more than it does now.

How Do Astronauts Cope with Less Gravity?

In space everything that is not tied down floats around the spacecraft! Living with little gravity can be fun, but astronauts have to get used to it. They train hard so they can learn to live and work in less gravity.

Life can be difficult. Shower water would float away, so astronauts need to clean themselves with wet towels. On spacewalks, astronauts must tie themselves to the spacecraft so they don't float away while they work. Astronauts usually sleep strapped to a wall with bungee cords so they can feel snug and secure!

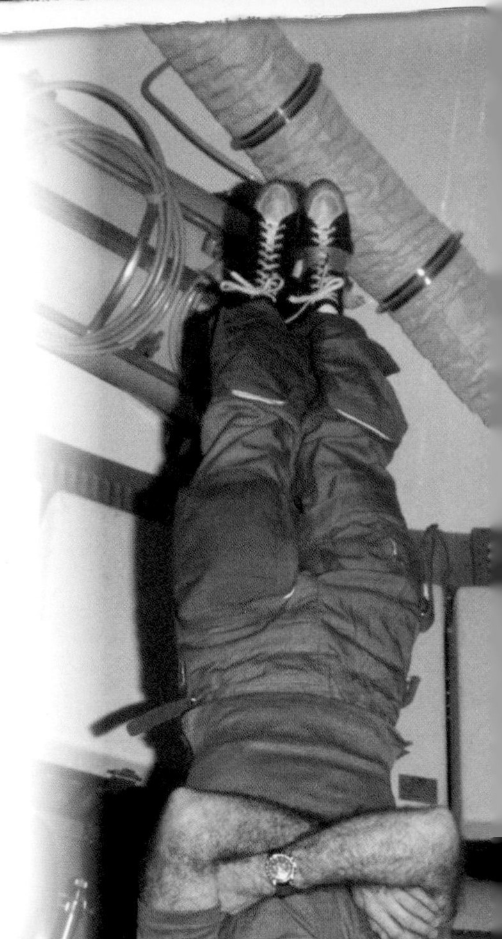

FACT FILE

Superstrength!

Some things are easier to do with less gravity. Objects that would be very heavy on Earth hardly weigh anything at all. Heavy equipment can be moved around easily in the spacecraft. In the photo on the right an astronaut in *Skylab 4* shows how easy it is to lift his friend using the tip of his finger!

Living with less gravity over a long period causes changes in the human body. Bones and muscles can become weak. There are changes in blood and fluid circulation. Some of these effects can be helped by exercising while in orbit.

An astronaut on board the International Space Station exercises strapped to a treadmill with bungee cords.

Astronauts train underwater. The conditions are very similar to working in space. This astronaut is practicing repairing the Space Shuttle. It must be very difficult holding the tools wearing thick gloves.

Do Astronauts Float or Free-Fall in Space?

Objects orbiting Earth are still pulled by Earth's gravity. Because they are in an orbit, they are moving sideways as well. This sideways force pulls objects away from Earth at the same time as Earth's gravity is pulling them down. Objects appear to float because they are falling at the same time as other objects in their surroundings. This free fall is known as **microgravity**.

Astronauts building the International Space Station as they fall in orbit through space over New Zealand!

The food in the photograph on the right is falling through space. Because both the food and the surrounding spacecraft are falling at the same speed and in the same direction, the food appears to be floating!

Astronaut's food appearing to float in microgravity

HANDS-ON SCIENCE

How Can You Stop Water from Flowing Out of a Hole?

You will need: a paper cup, some water, a sharp pencil

Make sure you do this experiment outside as it's messy! Using the pencil, poke a hole near the bottom of the outside of the cup. Fill the cup with water, keeping your finger over the hole. Take your finger off. A steady stream of water should pour out. The water is pulled down by gravity. Fill the cup again with your finger over the hole. Drop the cup and let go of the hole at the same time. Does the water still pour out of the side of the cup? When you drop the cup, the cup and water fall at the same speed, and are actually weightless as they fall. This time both the water and the cup are being pulled down at the same speed. This means that the water is still falling at the same rate, but so is the cup!

G-force measures the force of gravity on objects in space, and the force of **acceleration** an object feels anywhere. G-forces are often felt when you are riding on something fast that changes direction. Have you ever felt like you are being pushed into your seat when going up on a roller coaster, or around a corner in a fast car, or when a plane takes off? That feeling is caused by G-force.

When you go up a slope on a roller coaster you will weigh more! You may experience up to 4 Gs. That means you weigh 4 times more than usual. As you speed down again you weigh less than normal. Sometimes you weigh so little that you lift up into the air!

FACT FILE

Does an Object's Mass Affect its G-Force?

Sir Isaac Newton discovered that an object's mass affects the G-force that it feels. If two objects, one with a large mass and one with a small mass, experience the same acceleration, the object with the larger mass will feel more G-force. In the photo opposite the man will be experiencing much more of a change in forces on his roller coaster ride than the girl. Humans are able to bear G-forces of over 100 Gs for a split second, such as if they receive a slap on the face. Continuous G-forces above about 10 Gs can be deadly.

This young "Top Gun" would experience fewer Gs in his jet than an adult would.

HANDS-ON SCIENCE

Feel G-force at Work

You will need: a coin, some string, some tape, an open space

Tie some string around the coin and tape it very securely, so the coin can't slip out. Hold the coin by the string and feel its weight. That's its weight at 1 G. Now carefully start swinging the coin around in a circle like in the tennis ball gravity experiment on page 15. Does the coin feel any different? What about if you swing it faster? It may feel as much as 50 times heavier! Be careful when you slow down so the coin doesn't hit you on the head. That would hurt!

Could Gravity Cause an Object to Hit Earth?

If Earth's gravity attracts objects in space, could its gravity pull an object toward Earth? The answer is yes. In fact, many objects such as **asteroids** or **meteoroids** have hit Earth over the years. You can see craters in many parts of the world that have been made by such collisions.

An asteroid is a large, irregular-shaped object that orbits the Sun. A meteoroid is a piece of rock or metal that burns brightly, creating a fireball in the sky as it falls from outer space into Earth's atmosphere. Meteor Crater in Arizona was actually created by an asteroid. A meteorite is a piece of debris from an asteroid that falls to Earth. Most burst into many pieces when they enter Earth's atmosphere.

Meteor Crater, Arizona

FACT FILE

Fireballs That Occur in Earth's Atmosphere

The map below shows the small asteroid fireballs that have occurred between 1994 and 2013. The orange dots hit in the day, the blue dots hit at night. There were 255 day fireballs and 301 night fireballs!

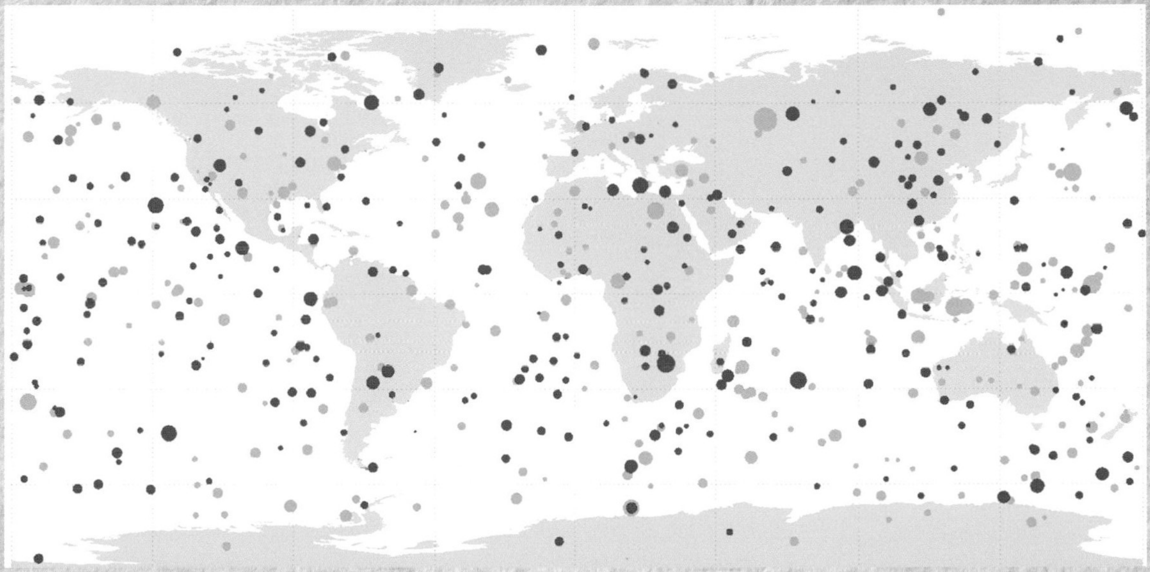

Impacts helped form our solar system. An object colliding with Earth is believed to have dislodged rock which formed the Moon. An impact 65 million years ago is believed to have killed off the dinosaurs. Throughout history, hundreds of Earth impacts have been reported. In Russia in 2013, the Chelyabinsk meteor event caused a large number of injuries and property damage. The Chelyabinsk meteor is the largest recorded object to have hit Earth since 1908.

The smoke trail of the Chelyabinsk fireball just before it hit Earth

Galaxy Quiz

Are you a galaxy genius? Test your skills with this quiz and see if you know your Newtons from your G-force!

1. Which of these statements is correct?
a) gravity causes objects to move toward each other
b) gravity causes objects to move away from each other

2. Which has the biggest gravitational pull?
a) the Sun
b) Earth
c) the Moon

3. Who discovered gravity?
a) Stephen Hawking
b) Albert Einstein
c) Sir Isaac Newton

4. What is mass?
a) how large something looks
b) how much matter something is made of
c) the weight of something

5. What could you measure with a Newton?
a) mass
b) size
c) weight

6. If you dropped a heavy ball and a light ball from a height, what would happen?
a) they would both hit the ground at the same time
b) the lighter ball would hit the ground first
c) the heavier ball would hit the ground first

7. You are shorter in the evening than in the morning?
a) true
b) false

8. What causes Earth's tides?
a) the Moon
b) the Sun
c) comets

9. G-force is?
a) a fuel used in spacecraft
b) a spacecraft
c) a measure of the force of gravity or acceleration

10. Objects often collide with Earth?
a) true
b) false

Glossary

acceleration (ak-SEH-luh-ray-shun)
An increase in speed by an object.

air resistance (EHR rih-ZIS-tens)
A drag of air on an object that causes it to slow down.

apparent weight (uh-PAH-rent WAYT)
A measure of downward force.

asteroids (AS-teh-roydz)
Bodies of rock and iron left over from when the main planets formed. They are in orbit around the Sun.

atmosphere (AT-muh-sfeer)
The gases around an object in space. On Earth this is air.

axis (AK-sis)
A straight line on which an object turns or seems to turn.

black hole (BLAK HOHL)
An invisible region believed to exist in space having a very strong gravitational field and thought to be caused by the collapse of a star.

condenses (kun-DENTS-es)
Cools and changes from a gas to a liquid.

distorts (dih-STORTS)
Twists out of a natural, normal, or original shape or condition.

equator (ih-KWAY-tur)
The imaginary line around Earth that separates it into two parts, northern and southern.

friction (FRIK-shin)
The rubbing of one thing against another.

gravitons (GRA-vih-tons)
Particles of the force of gravity that may or may not exist.

mass (MAS)
The amount of matter in something.

meteoroids (MEE-tee-uh-roydz)
Rocks in outer space that circle the Sun.

microgravity (my-kroh-GRA-vuh-tee)
A very small amount of gravity, the force that causes objects to move toward each other or feel like they have weight.

Newtons (NOO-tunz)
The scientific measure of force.

nuclear reactions (NOO-klee-ur ree-AK-shunz) Reactions, as in fission, fusion, or radioactive decay, that alter the energy, composition, or structure of an atomic nucleus.

orbit (OR-bit) A path an object takes around another object.

static electricity (STA-tik ih-lek-TRIH-suh-tee) An electrical charge within or on the surface of a material.

theories (THEE-reez) A group of ideas that tries to explain something.

Further Information

Books

Branley, Franklyn M. *Gravity Is A Mystery* (Let's Read and Find Out Science 2). New York, NY: HarperCollins, 2007.

Chin, Jason. *Gravity*. New York, NY: Roaring Brook Press, 2014.

Due to the changing nature of Internet links, PowerKids Press has developed an online list of websites related to the subject of this book. This site is updated regularly. Please use this link to access the list:
www.powerkidslinks.com/tgg/gravity

Index

A
acceleration 24, 25
air resistance 17
apparent weight 8
asteroids 11, 26, 27
astronauts 5, 20, 21, 22, 23

B
black holes 11, 12

C
Chelyabinsk meteor event 27

F
fireballs 26, 27

G
G-force 24, 25
Galilei, Galileo 17
gravitons 12
gravity 4, 5, 6, 7, 8, 10, 11, 12, 13, 15, 16, 17, 18, 19, 20, 21, 22, 23, 24, 25, 26

H
health 5, 21

I
International Space Station 22

M
mass 4, 8, 9, 12, 13, 14, 25
Meteor Crater 26
meteoroids 26
microgravity 22, 23
Moon, the 9, 18, 19

N
Newton, Sir Isaac 6, 12, 25
Newtons 9
nuclear reactions 10

O
orbits 14, 15, 22, 26

P
planets, other 10, 11

R
rotation of Earth 18, 19

S
stars 9, 10, 11
Sun, the 6, 16, 18

T
tides 18, 19

W
weightlessness 9, 20, 21

Answers

1. a)
2. a)
3. c)
4. b)
5. c)
6. a)
7. a)
8. a)
9. c)
10. a)